CONTENTS

ESSENTIAL ELEMENTS®

GUITAR ENSEMBLES

EARLY INTERMEDIATE

MULTICULTURAL SONGS

Arrangements by Peter Douskalis

ISBN 978-1-4950-6404-3

HAL•LEONARD®
CORPORATION

7777 W. BLUEMOUND RD. P.O. BOX 13819 MILWAUKEE, WI 53213

In Australia Contact:
Hal Leonard Australia Pty. Ltd.
4 Lentara Court
Cheltenham, Victoria, 3192 Australia
Email: ausadmin@halleonard.com.au

Visit Hal Leonard Online at
www.halleonard.com

INTRODUCTION

This collection of multicultural songs was created to provide teachers and students of guitar with a repertoire from around the globe and an entry point into the vast multicultural world of music. The arrangements presented within this book are all traditional, folk, or popular pieces from a wide range of countries and regions, yet all share musical commonalities. From harmonic relationships between the songs of Syria and Turkey, or Mexico and Russia; rhythmic commonalities between songs of Turkey and Greece; progression similarities in Armenian and South American music, as well as melodic consonants of Ireland and the Philippines, Cyprus and Iran, or Egypt and Japan; music is a universal language that unites us all.

As a public school educator in New York City and as a performing and recording artist, I have assembled these songs based on my own practice and work. Many of the melodies have been reharmonized with altered chord progressions in order to highlight a cross-cultural relationship between the songs, as well as to add modern flavors to these traditional pieces. By doing this, the arrangements are both multicultural and unique. It is meant to invoke the essence of the guitar while honoring the cultures' traditions.

Peter Douskalis

AINTE
(Sleep, My Child)
Smyrnan Folksong

CHARKI HIDJAZ
(The Sun Hangs High)
Turkish Folksong

DANNY BOY

Words by Frederick Edward Weatherly
Traditional Irish Folk Melody

DOOS YÁ LELLEE

Egyptian Folksong

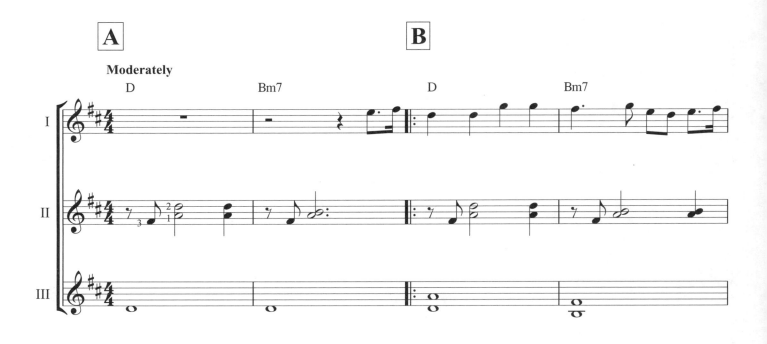

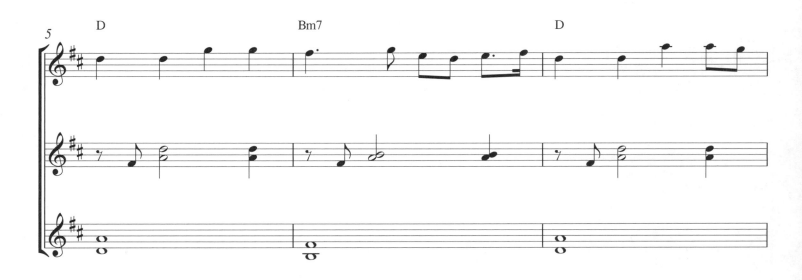

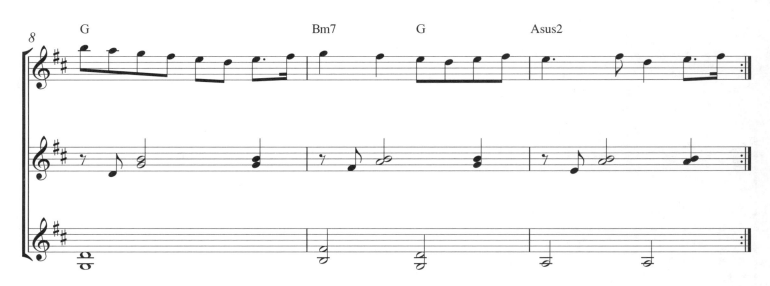

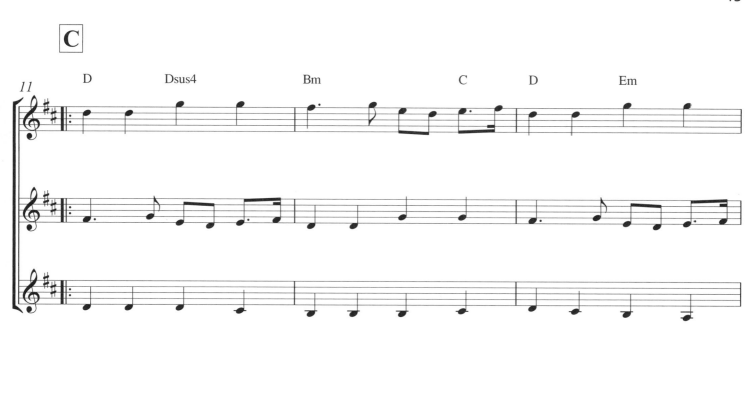

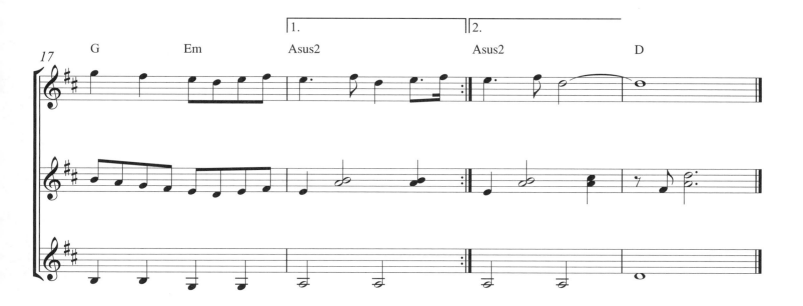

GUSCHI KI BEHAKK

Persian Folksong

JASMINE FLOWER SONG

Chinese Folksong

NOCHE SERENA

Mexican Folksong

O'ER THE DISTANT LONELY MOUNTAINS

Russian Folksong

PARUPARONG BUKID
(The Butterfly Field)
Traditional Filipino Folk Song

SAKURA
(Cherry Blossoms)
Traditional Japanese Folksong

SAMIOTISA
Traditional Greek Folk Song

LA MONTANÉRA

South American Folksong

SNAKE CHARMER

Traditional Indian

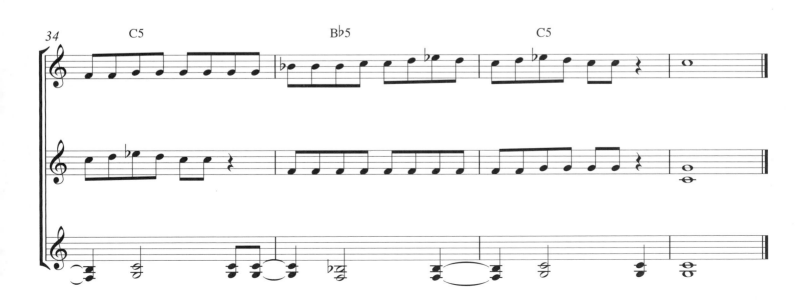

SOUFFLEZ UNE BRISE

Traditional Armenian Song by Komitas Vardapet

YASSEMÍ
Traditional Cypriot Love Song

ABOUT THE ARRANGER

Photo by Emily Rentz Photography

Peter Douskalis is a musician and educator who performs and records professionally, and is a music teacher for the New York City Department of Education. He has published his philosophy on multicultural music education curriculum design in the 30th World Conference Proceedings of the International Society for Music Education (ISME), and has further presented his philosophies in a TEDx Talk and at the 32nd ISME World Conference. Peter volunteers as President of the New York City Chapter of the charity Guitars Not Guns, and also contributes to projects for the organization Olympism For Humanity Alliance, Inc. His solo jazz guitar CD *The Dance of the Sea* has received national and international acclaim in *Just Jazz Guitar Magazine*, *Jazz Journal* (UK), *Cadence Magazine*, and *Los Angeles Jazz Scene*. He is a GHS Strings, Rocktron, and Steve Clayton Picks artist and uses Acoustic Image Amplifiers.

Visit him online at
www.douskalis.com

ESSENTIAL ELEMENTs FOR GUITAR

BOOK 1
Comprehensive Guitar Method
by Will Schmid and Bob Morris

Take your guitar teaching to a new level! With the time-tested classroom teaching methods of Will Schmid and Bob Morris, popular songs in a variety of styles, and quality demonstration and backing tracks on the accompanying CD, *Essential Elements for Guitar* is a staple of guitar teachers' instruction – and helps beginning guitar students off to a great start.

This method has been designed to meet the National Standards for Music Education, with features such as cross-curricular activities, quizzes, multicultural songs, basic improvisation and more. Concepts covered in Book 1 include: getting started; basic music theory; guitar chords; notes on each string; music history; ensemble playing; performance spotlights; and much more!

Songs used in Book 1 include such hits as: Dust in the Wind • Eleanor Rigby • Every Breath You Take • Hey Jude • Hound Dog • Let It Be • Ode to Joy • Rock Around the Clock • Stand by Me • Surfin' USA • Sweet Home Chicago • This Land Is Your Land • You Really Got Me • and more!

00862639 Book/CD Pack $17.99
00001173 Book Only $9.99

BOOK 2
Bob Morris

Essential Elements for Guitar, Book 2 is a continuation of the concepts and skills taught in Book 1 and includes all of its popular features as well – great songs in a variety of styles, a high-quality audio CD with demonstration and backing tracks, quizzes, music history, music theory, and much more. Concepts taught in Book 2 include: Playing melodically in positions up the neck; Playing movable chord shapes up the neck; Playing scales and extended chords in different keys; More right-hand studies – fingerpicking and pick style; Improvisation in positions up the neck; Studying different styles through great song selections; and more!

00865010 Book/CD Pack $17.99
00120873 Book Only $10.99

DAILY GUITAR WARM-UPS
by Tom Kolb
Mid-Beginner to Late Intermediate

This book contains a wide variety of exercises to help get your hands in top playing shape. It addresses the basic elements of guitar warm-ups by category: stretches and pre-playing coordination exercises, picking exercises, right and left-hand synchronization, and rhythm guitar warm-ups.

00865004 Book/CD Pack $9.99

Essential Elements Guitar Ensembles

The songs in the Essential Elements Guitar Ensemble series are playable by three or more guitars. Each arrangement features the melody, a harmony part, and bass line in standard notation along with chord symbols. For groups with more than three or four guitars, the parts can be doubled. This series is perfect for classroom guitar ensembles or other group guitar settings.

J.S. BACH
00123103 Early Intermediate Level..................$9.99

THE BEATLES
00865008 Early Intermediate Level..................$9.99

BOSSA NOVA
00865006 Intermediate/Advanced Level...............$9.99

CHRISTMAS CLASSICS
00865015 Mid-Intermediate Level $9.99

CHRISTMAS SONGS
00001136 Mid-Beginner Level $9.95

CLASSICAL THEMES
00865005 Late Beginner Level.........................$9.99

DISNEY SONGS
00865014 Early Intermediate Level...................$9.99

EASY POP SONGS
00865011 Mid-Beginner Level $9.99

DUKE ELLINGTON
00865009 Mid-Intermediate Level $9.99

GREAT THEMES
00865012 Mid-Intermediate Level $9.99

JIMI HENDRIX
00865013 Mid-Intermediate Level $9.99

JAZZ BALLADS
00865002 Early Intermediate Level...................$9.99

JAZZ STANDARDS
00865007 Mid-Intermediate Level $9.99

POP HITS
00001128 Late Beginner Level.........................$9.99

ROCK CLASSICS
00865001 Late Beginner Level.........................$9.95

ROCK INSTRUMENTALS
00123102 Mid-Intermediate Level $9.99

TOP HITS
00130606 Early Intermediate Level...................$9.99

Flash Cards

96 CARDS FOR BEGINNING GUITAR
00865000..$9.99

Essential Elements Guitar Songs

The books in the Essential Elements Guitar Songs series feature popular songs specially selected for the practice of specific guitar chord types. Each book includes eight great songs and a CD with fantastic sounding play-along tracks. Practice at any tempo with the included Amazing Slow Downer software!

POWER CHORD ROCK
Mid-Beginner Level
00001139 Book/CD Pack $12.99

OPEN CHORD ROCK
Mid-Beginner Level
00001138 Book/CD Pack $12.99

BARRE CHORD ROCK
Late Beginner Level
00001137 Book/CD Pack $12.99

FOR MORE INFORMATION, SEE YOUR LOCAL MUSIC DEALER, OR WRITE TO:

HAL•LEONARD®
CORPORATION
7777 W. BLUEMOUND RD. P.O. BOX 13819 MILWAUKEE, WI 53213

Prices, contents, and availability subject to change without notice.

HAL LEONARD GUITAR METHOD

by Will Schmid and Greg Koch

THE HAL LEONARD GUITAR METHOD is designed for anyone just learning to play acoustic or electric guitar. It is based on years of teaching guitar students of all ages, and it also reflects some of the best guitar teaching ideas from around the world. This comprehensive method includes: A learning sequence carefully paced with clear instructions; popular songs which increase the incentive to learn to play; versatility – can be used as self-instruction or with a teacher; audio accompaniments so that students have fun and sound great while practicing.

BOOK 1
00699010	Book	$7.99
00699027	Book with audio on CD & Online	$10.99
00155480	Deluxe Beginner Pack (Book/DVD/CD/Online Audio & Video/Poster)	$19.99

BOOK 2
00699020	Book	$7.99
00697313	Book/CD Pack	$10.99

BOOK 3
00699030	Book	$7.99
00697316	Book/CD Pack	$9.95

COMPOSITE
Books 1, 2, and 3 bound together in an easy-to-use spiral binding.
00699040	Books Only	$14.99
00697342	Book/3-CD Pack	$24.99

DVD
FOR THE BEGINNING ELECTRIC OR ACOUSTIC GUITARIST
00697318	DVD	$19.95
00697341	Book/CD Pack and DVD	$24.99

GUITAR FOR KIDS
A BEGINNER'S GUIDE WITH STEP-BY-STEP INSTRUCTION FOR ACOUSTIC AND ELECTRIC GUITAR
by Bob Morris and Jeff Schroedl
00865003	Book 1 – Book/CD Pack	$12.99
00697402	Songbook Book/CD Pack	$9.99
00128437	Book 2 – Book/Online Audio	$12.99

SONGBOOKS

EASY POP MELODIES
00697281	Book	$6.99
00697268	Book/CD Pack	$14.99

MORE EASY POP MELODIES
00697280	Book	$6.99
00697269	Book/CD Pack	$14.99

EVEN MORE EASY POP MELODIES
00699154	Book	$6.99
00697270	Book/Online Audio	$14.99

EASY POP RHYTHMS
00697336	Book	$6.95
00697309	Book/Online Audio	$14.99

MORE EASY POP RHYTHMS
00697338	Book	$6.95
00697322	Book/CD Pack	$14.95

EVEN MORE EASY POP RHYTHMS
00697340	Book	$6.95
00697323	Book/CD Pack	$14.95

EASY SOLO GUITAR PIECES
00110407	Book	$9.99

EASY POP CHRISTMAS MELODIES
00697417	Book	$6.99
00697416	Book/CD Pack	$14.99

LEAD LICKS
00697345	Book/Online Audio	$10.99

RHYTHM RIFFS
00697346	Book/Online Audio	$10.99

STYLISTIC METHODS

ACOUSTIC GUITAR
00697347	Book/Online Audio	$16.99
00697384	Acoustic Guitar Songs	$14.95

BLUEGRASS GUITAR
00697405	Book/CD Pack	$16.99

BLUES GUITAR
00697326	Book/Online Audio	$16.99
00697385	Blues Guitar Songs (with Online Audio)	$14.95

BRAZILIAN GUITAR
00697415	Book/CD Pack	$14.99

CHRISTIAN GUITAR
00695947	Book/CD Pack	$12.99
00697408	Christian Guitar Songs	$14.99

CLASSICAL GUITAR
00697376	Book/Online Audio	$14.99
00697388	Classical Guitar Pieces	$9.99

COUNTRY GUITAR
00697337	Book/CD Pack	$22.99
00697400	Country Guitar Songs	$14.99

FINGERSTYLE GUITAR
00697378	Book/CD Pack	$19.99
00697432	Fingerstyle Guitar Songs (with Online Audio)	$14.99

FLAMENCO GUITAR
00697363	Book/CD Pack	$14.99

FOLK GUITAR
00697414	Book/CD Pack	$14.99

JAZZ GUITAR
00695359	Book/Online Audio	$19.99
00697386	Jazz Guitar Songs	$14.95

JAZZ-ROCK FUSION
00697387	Book/CD Pack	$19.99

ROCK GUITAR
00697319	Book/Online Audio	$16.99
00697383	Rock Guitar Songs	$14.95

ROCKABILLY GUITAR
00697407	Book/CD Pack	$16.99

R&B GUITAR
00697356	Book/CD Pack	$16.99
00697433	R&B Guitar Songs	$14.99

REFERENCE

ARPEGGIO FINDER
00697351	9" x 12" Edition	$6.99

INCREDIBLE CHORD FINDER
00697200	6" x 9" Edition	$5.99
00697208	9" x 12" Edition	$6.99

INCREDIBLE SCALE FINDER
00695568	6" x 9" Edition	$5.99
00695490	9" x 12" Edition	$6.99

GUITAR CHORD, SCALE & ARPEGGIO FINDER
00697410		$19.99

GUITAR SETUP & MAINTENANCE
00697427	6" x 9" Edition	$14.99
00697421	9" x 12" Edition	$12.99

GUITAR TECHNIQUES
00697389	Book/CD Pack	$12.95

GUITAR PRACTICE PLANNER
00697401		$5.99

MUSIC THEORY FOR GUITARISTS
00695790	Book/Online Audio	$19.99

HAL•LEONARD® CORPORATION
7777 W. BLUEMOUND RD. P.O. BOX 13819 MILWAUKEE, WI 53213
www.halleonard.com

Prices, contents and availability subject to change without notice.